PRODUCTIVE
POWER HOUSE

Create the best version of yourself and
turn your direction towards success

Wisdom Walker

Contents

Productive Powerhouse

Create the best version of yourself and turn your direction towards success

Wisdom Walker

Chapter 1: Introduction

Chapter 1: Introduction

Productivity and Time Management

Ask any successful business or individual out there, and I'm sure they will tell you higher levels of productivity are a crucial aspect in ensuring revenue growth and achieving success.

In fact, many individuals and corporations willingly invest large sums of money and effort in order to improve in this area. Higher levels of productivity in individuals (whether as part of an organization or alone) helps to bring them closer to their success targets within a shorter time period, and prevents needless wastage of time, money and effort.

The dictionary defines productivity as "the quality, state, or fact of being able to generate, create, enhance, or bring forth goods and services". To explain it simply on a more individual level - it is just how much one can get done in a set period of time.

And when productivity is mentioned, time management is usually also brought up ; they go hand in hand. Both are strongly correlated - higher levels of productivity is usually the result of better time management.

All That You Know About Time Management Is Wrong

Yup, you got that right.

Your understanding of time management is very likely… wrong.

Time management is, in fact, a strange concept. Time cannot be managed or influenced; it is something that is pretty much out of our control. All of us, despite our social or financial background, are allocated 24 hours in a day, no more or less. Once gone, there's no way we can get it back.

Our day-to-day responsibilities - be it family or work, takes up a large portion of our time. Not only that, time is fleeting and so easily robbed from our hands. Unexpected things pop up all the time.
Priorities change. Things go terribly wrong. You get sick, or tired.

You can only do so much - you're only human, after all.

You can, however, control YOU. And your CHOICES. Time management is more correctly, all about self-discipline and task management. It's the management of expectations as well as interruptions. It is the ability to manage your actions, habits and priorities based on the time you are given. It is understanding what matters most, making a choice to make room for that in your life, and getting rid of the unnecessary, unimportant stuff that's hogging up your valuable time.

Also, time management is not a one system fits all method. There is no perfect method. Different individuals have different styles - we're all wired differently in terms of personality type, identity and individual life circumstances. Some may find that a to-do list works for them; others may find to-do lists hard to follow and demotivating. It's all about finding your groove - different strokes for different folks.

Multitasking because you want to manage time better? Bad idea. Contrary to popular belief, faster and more is NOT always better. Multitasking is one way to destroy your productivity levels.

Sure... you seem to get more done this way.

However, you are probably more likely to make mistakes - which will result in you doing things over again. Stick to focusing on one task at a time, and taking sufficient breaks whenever possible - you'll stand to accomplish more this way. Now, we've mentioned that juggling multiple tasks at one time is counterproductive. However, striving to complete each task no matter how long it takes is also not a wise idea when it comes to time management. Restrict your time spent on a task, and schedule accordingly.

As you can see, a lot of what we know regarding time management are in fact, myths. Many of us have skewed perceptions or are misinformed when it comes to time management. These myths, over time, through the people around us or the media we consume, become deeply ingrained within our mindsets; we eventually regard them as facts and hold on to them. As a result, we are prevented from becoming truly and fully productive in any aspect of our lives.

Chapter 2:
The Big E's

Chapter 2: The Big E's

Effectiveness versus efficiency.

Both terms are adjectives that begin with the letter 'e' and are used to describe how work is done. Not only that, but they also sound quite similar.

It is relatively easy to mistake one for the other or use them interchangeably (a lot of people do!). However, these terms are anything but similar - in fact, they each carry completely different meanings.

Effectiveness is all about doing the right things; it is result oriented. It is when one's objectives are in line with their main goals, and indirectly your purpose.

It is finding ways to improve outcomes. For example, if your goal is to increase awareness and sales of a particular product to reach a particular target, you should engage in tasks or activities that will help move you closer to your goals (eg. marketing and ads, in this scenario) , and not waste time on irrelevant tasks that do not serve your goals. This makes you effective.

Efficiency, however, is more about doing things right; this aspect is task oriented. It is using better ways to get something done well in the shortest amount of time possible, while utilizing the least amount of resources and/or costs. An example of efficiency would be using a computerized system to get things done accurately in a shorter span of time; as opposed to relying on manual methods to do the same thing, which is susceptible to human error and is more time consuming.

Either one can exist without the other; one can be effective but not efficient, and vice versa. It is entirely possible for one to be effective in achieving their goals, while being inefficient in the way they do it. It is also entirely possible to be none of both at all.

In fact, there are four possibilities:

1. Effective and Efficient

2. Effective and Inefficient

3. Ineffective and Efficient

4. Ineffective and Inefficient

It should be noted however that true, optimal productivity is a combination of both efficiency and effectiveness (Number 1) - the Holy Grail for every individual or organization.

It is not possible for an organization or person to reach peak productivity
levels, if they are lacking in either efficiency or effectiveness (Number 2, 3
and 4). If anything, they're setting themselves up for either mediocrity or inevitable failure.

Effectiveness > Efficiency

In terms of order of importance, effectiveness should be prioritized over efficiency in all your considerations about productivity.

This however does not mean that you should disregard the importance of efficiency altogether - again, as mentioned earlier, productivity is a balanced combination of both.
Effectiveness involves the big picture. Putting effectiveness first just means that you should first and foremost focus on doing the right things in order to improve your chances of getting a good outcome.

Once you get yourself on track and laid out the basics, you can then look into how you can improve the way you do things. The logic here is to concentrate on being efficient at the tasks which are significant and are effective in contributing to your goals.
There's no point in being particularly efficient when the tasks you carry out do not contribute to your purpose and goals.

To sum things up: efficiency is a modifier for effectiveness, not a substitute.

Efficiency is meaningless on its own.

The problem with most people is that they tend to gravitate towards efficiency, rather than effectiveness. It is perfectly understandable - being efficient is a whole lot easier than being effective. Being efficient involves improvements on a smaller, more manageable scale; effectiveness however requires a whole lot of brainstorming about one's goals, values and different approaches, on a larger scale. And that is intimidating.

Not only that, people who put efficiency before effectiveness have this tendency of looking for better and perfect ways of doing things, and head nowhere instead - which ironically, leads to ineffectiveness.

Increasing Effectiveness

So how does one increase their effectiveness?

Put some time aside to evaluate these few things:

- Clarify the What- focusing on the results you want to achieve and define the picture of success.

- Clarify and pursue key strategies that will give you the highest possibility for success.

Now that you've established your plan of action, you can focus on how to increase your efficiency. This would mean concentrating on the How's - implementation of your strategies in the most efficient way possible, and improving how you do things as you go along.

In the coming chapters, we will look into further detail on this, as well as many other helpful tips that will skyrocket your productivity to optimum levels.

Chapter 3:
The Success Journey

Chapter 3: The Success Journey

To embark on a major journey, you should first have a real idea of your destination.

This way, you'll be able to plan adequately for your journey -directions, mode of transport, estimated costs, time, etc.

Skip that, and you'd end up wandering aimlessly. Or find yourself lost somewhere in the middle of Timbuktu. Sure, you're on a journey alright...but where?

Similarly, when it comes to planning for your success, you will need a "destination" and a "roadmap". That would be a clear vision of what you want, and specific goals to help you on your way to achieve your idea of success.

Creating A Vision

To be truly effective in your pursuit for success, you should first be able to visualize your "destination" - a clear vision of where you want to be in the future. It's what you desire, your passion, your purpose in doing something.

Creating a vision is important. It's the very thing that gives you direction, a compass that directs you in making the best decisions, and taking the right actions that will propel you towards success. It's what gets you excited and motivated to push beyond your self-imposed boundaries. It's what keeps you focused and on top of the game.

To begin, take some time to envision how you see your life in your ideal future. Reflect on your passions, core principles and values you live by, and your purpose in life.

Remember to define your vision - make sure your vision is specific and clear. It is your starting point - the very foundation you will be building on. It is the ideal you will be striving for, to get close to.

It should be something that is in line with your values and principles, as well as your view of the future. Simply coming up with a vague vision of wanting to be "wealthy" or "popular" is not enough ; it should be something more solid and specific.

You can also think of the people you admire and look up to - the kind of characteristics or habits you wish to emulate yourself. In fact, you can even ask them to be your mentor, to help you think things through on certain areas and advise you on what has worked for them.

Again, don't restrain yourself too much when creating your own vision. Your vision is personal and unique - there is no right or wrong. It's something that only you can decide for yourself, and this also is dependent on what you want to achieve in life.

Remember, the point of creating a vision is to know your reason for doing something, and to help you be more focused and motivated.

Setting Your Goals

But simply envisioning the future is not enough - that just reduces your vision to little more than a glorious daydream.

Visions will remain unattainable when not coupled with goals. And this is where goals come in.

Goals are more specific and quantifiable targets - it's the "roadmap" to your journey of success. They act as benchmarks or milestones, aiding you in laying the path for the rightful achievement of your vision. This also includes the tactics as well as strategies you use to work towards your vision.

To explain it simply, goals are a tool to help you take conscious steps each day to help you realize your vision.

Again, I have to emphasize here that a solid, clear vision first is important. The goals you set and work towards achieving should be in line with your vision. This keeps you focused on the big picture as to why you should complete your goals.

A good approach to use when it comes to setting your goals

is the S.M.A.R.T.E.R approach to goal setting.

S.M.A.R.T.E.R is an acronym that stands for:

Specific

Measurable

Achievable

Relevant

Time Bound

Evaluation

Revise

Here's a detailed elaboration of this approach.

1. Specific

Your goal should be specific and crystal clear - you should be able to know what success looks like here. The more specific you can get, the better. A good tip here is to ask yourself the 5 W questions below :

- What do I want to accomplish?
- Why is this goal important?
- Who is involved?
- Where is it located?
- Which resources or limits are involved?

2. Measurable

The goals you set for yourself should be measurable and quantifiable. This is so you can track your progress and performance properly. Being able to see progress is a great motivator - it gets you excited knowing that you are well on your way to success. Not only that, this helps your focus.

3. Achievable

A successful goal should be one that is realistic and achievable. Lying to yourself and aiming for a goal that is beyond your abilities will only result in failure to reach that goal.

That being said - this is not an excuse for you to be complacent here. You should set goals that will stretch your abilities but also remain possible for you to achieve.

Also, you should consider factors that will affect the achievability of the goal, like financial and time constraints.

4. Relevant

Your goal should be relevant. It should matter to you, and also be aligned with your other goals and vision. This step keeps you from focusing on the wrong things.

5. Time-Bound

Every goal you set should have a deadline - this gives you something to work towards. However, aiming to hit a goal in 5 to 7 years is not considered a proper deadline. Sure, it contains a time element - but it's not specific enough.

Your plan to reach a goal in 5 years will be quite different from your plan to reach a goal within 7 years.

Setting a more specific date for your goals allows you to develop a clearer plan to achieve it. This also prevents you from letting other everyday matters take priority over your goals.

6. Evaluate

Over time, things happen and goals change. Look over your goals from time to time and evaluate them ; check if they need changing to fit your current situation. Constant evaluation of you goals is essential for you to reach your goals.

7. Revise

Upon evaluation, if you find that your goals need readjusting, revise them accordingly.

Chapter 4:
The Success Action Plan

ACTION PLAN

Chapter 4: The Success Action Plan

Every success story comes from perfect planning. It is harder to achieve success from simply going at it and hoping for the best. This is because you might encounter problems along the way and don't have any ways to overcome it.

It is baffling why some succeed and some fail. Sometimes it may even seem unfair. You may know friends and family who are fantastic people, act appropriately, have good education, have good jobs, lead good families and generally possess the good things in life. But somehow they still wallow in desperation and difficulty.

Then there are those who always achieve so much success and yet do not have high merits. They have no education, poor attitude about themselves and other people and maybe dishonest and unethical. In these cases, the actual defining factor is the strength of one's desire to get ahead.

Despite their lack of virtues, knowledge and appreciation, these people often get ahead in the success race. This is also why many times you see drug dealers and gang members driving Lamborghinis, while many good and honest people you know are struggling to pay their bills. If the desire is strong enough to achieve the goals, why do many still not?

The sad answer is there is only desire, but no work. Oftentimes many dream big but do not hustle and put in the work. They do not stay up late at night developing new solutions to their problems.
They do not work 16 hours a day closing a sale. They do not struggle to ensure the prospects they approach turn into qualified clients.
They do not learn all that they possibly can about our industry and our markets. They do not work to get around the right sources of influence, or to associate with those people who can help them to achieve their goals. While you are sitting there dreaming, some are getting off their seats and working.

So, what are the steps to develop a plan that will work amazingly and take you to the finish line strongly? Here are the five major points to keep in mind:

Step 1: Develop The Right Plan For You.

Some people are very detail-oriented and are able to closely follow an intricate plan to the letter. Others are more effective when they see the bigger picture first and then frame out the small steps that lead to the final goal.

Each of us is unique and motivated by different factors and you've got to develop a plan that is right for you and fits you. Some plans will not be as intricate as others, but we all must have a plan, along with goals in that plan, to move us along. If you are a free spirit, don't tell yourself you are going to spend two hours a day with a book and a journal. It probably won't happen and you will just get discouraged. Whatever your personality, your strengths and your weaknesses, develop the plan around them. This is not a one-plan-fits-all proposition.

If you're detail-oriented, it's best to map out the small steps in your plan with utmost focus. This means being very clear on what you want to achieve daily, weekly or monthly. For example, the first small step to achieving your ideal weight is to cut out 1 serving of sweetened drinks by the end of Week 1.

For those who like to see the bigger picture first, it helps if you imagine how it will be if you're, say, 20 pounds lighter. You may be able to get out of bed easier, your energy level will rise, and you will fit into those apparels that you yearn to wear. Then, map out what you need to do in order to achieve that.

Step2: Allocate The Time For It.

This is crucial in your planning, because you'll be clearer on when you should commit to achieving your goals. In this case, let's use back the weight-loss goal.

It might be alternating aerobics and weight training every other weekend. It might be running 30 minutes each morning or swimming after work. It might be in the car listening to weight loss motivational podcasts on your way to work, or it might even be meeting your coach once a week to set your workout plan and to check on your progress.

Whatever it is, be specific on the where, when and how to do it, and actually do it. In your step-by-step plan, put down points that represents small achievable goals that you can accomplish in a short time. They should be specific because if you straightaway put down a major goal, you may think it's too big to achieve.

The next crucial element in achieving your goals to success is not starting to work on it, but to keep going at it. Discipline comes into important play here. Take those steps every day, which will close the gap to your goals.

Step 3: Keep A Journal

Two words that will help you a lot: Take Notes. In all seriousness, your memory should not be trusted. It's much better and workable when you write it down, and write it in a single place so it's easier for you to remind yourself where you're heading to and what success have you achieved. You will find that this step will help you tremendously in the long run.

Record everything! Be it the ideas and inspiration or reminders and failures that you have gone through. This massively helps carry you from where you are to where you want to be. Write down the ideas that you get from outside sources that impact you most.

Complement them with your own ideas that further suit your style. Do a brainstorm session with yourself on what you want and how you want to do it. And finally, record all your dreams and ambitions, and put it where you'll read them first so you stay reminded and motivated.

Your journals are a gathering place for all the valuable information that you will find. If you come across something that you think will hugely help you achieve, for example, wealth, power, sophistication, health, influence, culture or uniqueness, do not delay. Write it down. Strengthen your reflection and motivation by using the information you gather and put it where it will be recorded permanently.

Step 4: Reflect on Where You Are and Where You Want To Be

Next step is to make time for reflection. This is where you spend some time to go back over, to study again the things you've learned and the things you've done each day. This can also be called 'running the tapes again' so the day locks firmly in your memory and serves as a tool for motivation and keeps you going.

As you go through it, spend time reflecting on its significance to you. What you can do is take a few minutes at the end of each day before you go to sleep, and go back over what happened and you have achieved during the day: pay extra attention to who you talked to, who you saw, what they said, what happened and how you felt.

Another way is to take a longer time at the end of the week to reflect on the week's activities and achievements. It also pays to periodically stop, step back and look at what you're doing and see if it serves to push you to your goal or otherwise. Then tweak it a bit so you are kept on track. Take a half day at the end of the month and a weekend at the end of the year so that you've got it, so that it never disappears, to ensure that the past is even more valuable and will serve your future well.

Step 5: Set Clear and Achievable Goals

Remember that your plan is the roadmap that shows the way to your goals, which means it is always an essential tool that helps you to succeed. Setting goals is also an invaluable skill to learn because it can change your life for the better, and does it in the fastest way.

Mastering this unique process can have a powerful effect on your life, too. If you have a set of clearly defined goals, it can surprisingly be a powerful indication of telling if you have only hundreds of dollars or millions in the bank! If you don't have them yet, better to frame them out immediately so you have a lucid view of your future and dreams. Set your own goals clearly as soon as possible because it is the greatest influence on your future and the greatest force that will pull you in the direction that they want to go. It all boils down to this: If you plan and design your goals well, your future will be very bright.

Step 6: Act on It!

So what still holds you back from your success? You have a very strong desire to do it already, and you have already created a plan that will take you there.

The **next** step?

Take action! Here's the thing: successful people aren't necessarily smarter than others; they just work the plan to the letter, they follow through on the plan and ensure the plan serves them to reach greater heights.

The best time to act on your plan is when your emotions are strong. There's a little thing called The Law of Diminishing Intent. This essentially means your desires diminish over time, and if you don't act immediately after having the desire, your goals are harder to achieve.

Act when the idea strikes you, when the emotion is high, but if we delay and we don't translate that into action fairly soon, the intention starts to diminish, diminish and a month from now its cold and a year from now it can't be found. This is where discipline comes to play - work the plan when the idea is strong, clear and powerful. You must capture the emotion and put it into disciplined activities and translate it

into strong unrelenting action.

Chapter 5:
Becoming A Productive Powerhouse

Chapter 5: Becoming a Productive Powerhouse

High productivity is a major goal for many people, because more things can get done if you are in a high-productivity environment. While this concept may seem simple, to fully understand what it means to increase productivity, the definition cannot be taken literally. You actually must develop a stronger understanding of this concept wholly and use it to your advantage fully.

To put it in simple terms high productivity means that you are putting out products more quickly or completing tasks at higher speed than before. Theoretically, it made sense - the more products someone produces or services the person completes, the more positive results come in, making increased productivity a high priority for many workplace environments.

There are some things, however, that studies say cause your productivity at work to plummet, such as unfavorable environment, distractions and plain old procrastination.

You cannot always control your environment, but the good news is you can control what you get done. Plus, you can learn from others to be even more productive. There are probably more direct ways to help your productivity increase such as a conducive environment or closing the Facebook tab on your browser, But these are small hacks that actually only do so much. There are more meaningful ways to be your best. And you can learn these skills by taking some cues from the world's most successful people.

Have Big Goals in Mind

Firstly, you can set big goals and then act to fully accomplish them.
Facebook founder Mark Zuckerberg is a master at this, making room
each year for a new challenge, which he says allows him to "learn new
things and grow outside my work at Facebook." And it pays!
He's now fluent in Mandarin and is meeting new people all the time.
Looking at it backwards can help too, link Amazon's Jeff Bezos does.
He makes room for big goals by starting with the customer's needs and
working backward to build skills to get that work done faster.
As Bezos said it, "We learn whatever skills we need to service the
customer. We build whatever technology we need to service the
customer."

Give Each Day A Theme

Try copying CEO Jack Dorsey for this. When splitting his time
between Square and Twitter, he stays productive by giving each day a
theme -- Mondays for management, Tuesdays for product, etc. As he
explains, "There is interruption all the time, but I can quickly deal with
an interruption and then know that it's Tuesday, I have product
meetings, and I need to focus on product stuff."

Another tip you can use is the "no-meeting Wednesdays" Facebook
co-founder Dustin Moskovitz believes that this gives him and his team
a good amount of time each week for "focused, heads-down work."

Set Limits

You can only spend so much time focusing on something. After that, It's time to move on to the next important thing. For example, former Nissan CEO Carlos Ghosn sets only allocates 1 and a half hours to on single-purpose, non-operational meetings, with half the time for presentation and the other half for discussions.

Another thing you can limit is the length of your emails. The Facebook COO Sheryl Sandberg says she responds to every single work email, but she saves time by keeping the responses short. "I would rather give a short, quick, incomplete answer than wait and do it better," she says.

Deep Work Zone

Focus, focus, focus. This is perhaps most important productivity secret. Bill Gates would set time for Deep Work, where he would allocate time each week to do his most challenging work without any distractions -- no stopping, not even for sleep. Cal Newport, author of The book "Deep Work" said, "Deep work is important ... not because distraction is evil, but because it enabled Bill Gates to start a billion-dollar industry in less than a semester."

Streamline Decisions

Jeff Bezos makes a lot of decisions every day. Since this can be time-consuming, he's developed a four-step process for navigating his business more quickly. First, One-size-fits-all decisions are a no-no. "Many decisions are reversible, two-way doors," he writes in his letter to shareholders. "Those decisions can use a light-weight process.

"Second, make the decision when you are at 70% of your intended information. "If you wait for 90% ...you're probably being slow," he writes.

Disagree and commit. "This phrase will save a lot of time," he writes. "If you have conviction on a particular direction even though there's no consensus, it's helpful to say, 'Look, I know we disagree on this but will you gamble with me on it? Disagree and commit?' By the time you're at this point, no one can know the answer for sure, and you'll probably get a quick yes."

And fourth, address the real misalignments early and focus on them immediately. "Sometimes teams have different objectives and fundamentally different views," he writes. "They are not aligned. No amount of discussion, no number of meetings will resolve that deep misalignment. Without escalation, the default dispute resolution mechanism for this scenario is exhaustion."

Get To Work Before Everyone Else

The early bird catches the worm. Try starting work before everyone wakes. Like 4 am like Sallie Krawcheck, CEO of thc digital financial platform Ellevest. The reason is "The most precious commodity in business is time. And I find I am most productive when I balance time that I spend with others with blocks of time during which I can think, write and —my favorite — build earnings models," she writes.

She further elaborated that at this time, "My mind is clear, not yet caught
up in the multiple internal conversations that we all conduct with ourselves once we gear up for our first meeting of the day. And there's a peace that comes from knowing that my family is all in bed and safe

upstairs while I work. It is at this time of day that I often have a rush of ideas (some of them are actually good)."

Protect Your Time

Instead on starting the day with important tasks, Keller Williams Realty founder Gary Keller blocks out the first few hours of his day to work on his most important task for the year—his "one thing."

This is because this one thing, when tackled, will make everything easier to do or unnecessary. Keller has used this to write books and grow his company to the largest real estate franchise. Keller also believes that until this one thing is done, anything else can impair it. "The key is time. Success is built sequentially. It's one thing at a time," he writes in "The One Thing: The Surprisingly Simple Truth behind Extraordinary Results".

Close Virtual Doors

Open work environments opens up many good possibilities but also can hinder productivity with unnecessary distractions and interruptions. Michael Pryor, former CEO of Trello, encourages workers to close virtual doors by turning off Slack and email, and by putting a Post-It note on their desk that says "heads down."

Interruptions are weird. They leech time from important projects and take a while to recover from. "Every time you switch contexts, there's this huge cost associated with that," Pryor said in an interview with

Time. "Our time is limited, essentially. Your trick is to be able to ration that resource for all the things you need to do, and that's the hardest part of being productive."

Separate Work And Personal Life

This may seem counterintuitive or even obvious to some, but it's nonetheless as important as anything. YouTube CEO Susan Wojcicki makes being home in time for dinner with family a priority. Leaving the office on time helps her consolidates her work and get it done more rapidly, so when she is home, she can focus on her family without any distractions.

"We try to have the rule to not check email between 6 p.m. and 9 p.m., because if you are on your phone then it's hard to disconnect," Wojcicki said in an interview with the Wall Street Journal.

Pulling the plug when the time comes can actually help you stay productive, creative and your pursuit to succeed a surety.

"[Success] is not based on the number of hours that you've worked," Wojcicki says. "If you are working 24/7, you're not going to have any interesting ideas."

Clear Out Your Inbox Everyday

"Email is unidirectional—anyone, at any time, can just go to your inbox without permission, invitation or consideration, Elliot Weissbluth, CEO of HighTower, writes on LinkedIn. "Empowering the world to demand a thin slice of your attention is more than unfair— it's a recipe for constant distraction."

He uses three rules to simplify things and keep him focused and productive

1. Unsubscribe from newsletters. It takes more time than simply deleting, but actually saves hours every year.

2. Delete and completely forget about it. "When in doubt, delete. If it's that important, someone will follow up with you. Then respond to what you can and move the rest to recycling" he writes.

3. Don't bother filing. Use a good search tool to scan your folders and find things you need instantly.

"If you do nothing else but these three things, your inbox will be a lot leaner," he writes. "Whatever messages are left become a to-do list of the items that actually need your care and attention. Keep this list short, between two and five items, or what you can actually hope to achieve on any given day. Get those items done and you've just reached Inbox Zero."

It might seem unorthodox that some steps make you seem less productive. But again, it is more than simply cranking out more than you usually do. Being productive is not only being efficient. It also means you are effective in your work, where you take steps to completely turn problems into solutions that make extra work unnecessary.

Chapter 6: Your Energy

Chapter 6: Your Energy

To effectively re energize yourself, you need to shift your emphasis from to investing more in yourself, so you stay motivated and able to bring more to the table. You need to recognize energy-depleting behaviors and then take active steps in changing them or deleting them altogether.

Energy is very important when you're aiming for high productivity. If you look at successful people and ask them how they do it, they will always say energy as one of their main drives to success.
Defined in physics as the capacity to work, energy comes from four main sources in you: your body, emotions, mind, and spirit.

The Body

It is no news that improper nutrition, exercise, sleep, and rest affect your energy levels, emotion management and focus. Nonetheless, you may be guilty of ignoring ways to practice healthy behaviors, given all the other demands in your life.

You may be doing things such as skipping breakfast, failing to express appreciation to others, struggling to focus on one thing at a time, or spending too little time on activities that give them a sense of purpose. While it is not surprising that these behaviors are counterproductive, having them all listed in one place can become uncomfortable, sobering, and galvanizing. This may sound harsh, but is actually a necessary first step to restoring your body energy.

The next step is to identify rituals for building and renewing physical energy. Gary Faro, a vice president at Wachovia was significantly overweight, ate poorly, lacked a regular exercise routine, worked long hours, and typically slept no more than five or six hours a night.

Faro began exercising with cardio and strength training. He also starts to go to bed at a regular time and sleep longer. He changed his meals from two big ones a day to small meals every three hours. The aim is to stabilize glucose levels over the course of the day, avoiding peaks and valleys.

And the result?

Faro lost 50 pounds and his energy levels soared.

Another way to restore energy is taking brief, regular breaks at specific intervals throughout the workday. We have "Ultradian rhythms" which refers to 90- to 120-minute cycles during which our bodies swing through high and low energy states. At the end of each cycle, the body displays a need of recovery like restlessness, yawning, hunger, and being unfocused. Usually this gets ignored and in turn burns down your energy reservoir faster.

If done properly, intermittent breaks can increase and sustain performance. It is possible to recover well in a short time if it involves a ritual that allows you to separate briefly from work and let your mind rest. You can talk to a colleague about something other than work, listen to music, or walk up and down stairs.

The Emotion

When you can take more control of your emotions, you can massively improve the quality of your energy. To do this, you must become aware of how you feel at various points of time and its effect on your effectiveness.

People tend to perform best when they're feeling positive energy, and won't perform well vice versa. Unfortunately, people tend to slip into negative emotions and trigger their fight-or-flight mechanism when met with relentless demands and unexpected challenges. The signs may be irritability, impatience, anxiety and insecurity. These are big culprits in draining your energy.

One ritual for erasing negative emotions is "buying time". You can take deep abdominal breaths and exhale slowly for 10 seconds to relax and recover, and defuse your fight-or-flight response.

Expressing appreciation to others is a practice which is as beneficial to the giver as to the receiver. It can take the form of a handwritten note, an email, a call, or a conversation. The more detailed and specific the appreciation given, the higher the impact. To achieve higher success at doing this, like any other rituals, set aside some time to do it.

Finally, you can change the stories you tell yourself about the events in your life. You can see this often, people casting themselves in the role of a victim instead of being thankful for what they have.

This is powerful because you are more aware of the difference between the facts and the way you interpret it. This may seem obvious but you can actually discover that you have a choice about how to view something and recognize how powerfully your story influences your emotions.

To change a perception to a story you want to tell, view it through any of three alternatives, represented by lenses. With the reverse lens, ask yourself what the others involved will say and are they actually true. With the long lens, look at how it impacts you in the future. With the wide lens, ask yourself how you can improve and learn from this.

The Mind

Multitasking, while sounding and looking cool, actually undermines productivity. This is because a temporary shift in attention from one task to another increases the amount of time to finish a task by as much as 25%. You are likelier to be more efficient to fully focus for 90 to 120 minutes, take a true break, and then fully focus on the next activity. This focus and break cycle is called "Ultradian Sprints".

Once you can see how much you struggle to concentrate, you can combat this by creating rituals to reduce the interruptions that bother you. Start out with an exercise that makes you face the impact of your daily distractions.

A real-life example is from Dan Cluna, a vice president at Wachovia, who
designed 2 rituals to increase focus. The first one is to leave his desk and go into a conference room whenever he has a task that requires concentration to stop distractions from phone calls.

The result is he finishes reports in a third of the time. The second is by not picking up any phone calls in meetings with the people who report to him. This is because it stretched the time of the meetings and cost his full attention. He now only answers the voice-mail messages in his downtime.

Here's another method to Instead of replying your emails as soon as they come in, set time to answer them at specific times of the day. This actually can allow you to clear your inbox faster if you fully focus on your emails for 45 minutes at a time.

Another way to mobilize mental energy is to focus systematically on activities that impact you the most in the long term. Identify the most important challenge for the next day and make it their very first priority when you arrive at work in the morning.

The Spirit

Your spirit is at your highest when your work and activities are consistent with what you value and have a sense of meaning and purpose the most. If the work you're doing really matters to you, you will have more energy, focus, and perseverance.

However, the demands and pace of corporate life don't leave much space for these issues, and many don't even know that meaning and purposes are potential sources of energy. When you experience the value of the rituals you establish, you can start to see that being attentive to your own needs intensely influences their effectiveness and satisfaction at work.

Give yourself the opportunity to ask questions about what really mattered to you. You will find that these will be both illuminating and energizing. This can be highly important and thoughtful because it will really make you aware of what you want to be really remembered for.

To access the energy of the human spirit, you need to clarify priorities and establish rituals in three categories:

1. Doing what you do best and enjoy most at work;

2. Consciously allocating time and energy to the areas of your life, like work, family, health, service to others that you deem most important;

3. And living your core values in your daily behaviors.

Chapter 7: Powerhouse Productivity Hacks

Chapter 7: Powerhouse Productivity Hacks

There are 5 hacks you can employ in order to be on top of your productivity game:

1. Having A Game Plan

The basic principle of productivity is having a game plan. This is accomplished by having effective time-management. If you do not have a game-plan for getting it done, the results will not be satisfying. While procrastination and wasting time impede productivity, lack of effective time-management can be as destructive.

Increasing your productivity and getting things done means having a good game-plan. First, you need to know exactly what must be done. Second, even if you do not have a specific deadline, you must also decide when it must be done. The third step is putting yourself to the task of doing it.

You want to accomplish your goals, whether they are short-term or long-term. You also want to be proud of and satisfied with the results. When you are not content to simply "go with the flow," and instead take your game-plan seriously every step of the way, you are nearly guaranteed of success, pride, and satisfaction.

Here are the 3 components of an effective game plan:

- Identify What Needs To Be Done

Firstly, you need to know exactly what needs to be done. For instance, if you have been assigned to prepare for a presentation as well as a meeting that will be held within the week. You have to be clear of the tasks at hand.

- Decide When It Must Be Done (Timeline)

Secondly, even if you do not have a specific deadline, you must set a timeframe for the task to be completed. When you have organized your workload, you are less likely to procrastinate and this will help you in prioritizing your tasks as well as managing your time.

- Do It

The third step is putting yourself to the task of doing it. There's no use of all the planning and organizing if you do not take immediate action in completing the tasks.

2. What Should You Do First?

If you think about back when you were in school, you may remember teachers telling you that the best way to approach homework and other projects was to do the hardest task first. They may have also advised you to tackle the homework subject you dislike the most first, before moving on. This same approach can greatly enhance your productivity today.

Always start with a difficult task. When you begin your day, regardless at work or if you have countless assignments to be submitted before exams, try and put this approach to action.

Instead of beginning with a task you enjoy, or one which comes easily to you, start with one you dislike, or one which you feel will be quite difficult. At the end of the day, you may be pleasantly surprised with how much you have accomplished. You will also feel that the day has gone much smoother.

The explanation for this is because usually at the start of your day, you have more energy as compared to the end of the day. When you devote this energy to the hardest or most disliked tasks, you will not feel as drained or frustrated in doing them. Secondly, if you begin with the easier tasks at hand first, you will be looking at your difficult upcoming tasks with negativity. This will no doubt cause your motivation to decline and you will dread the rest of your day.

This approach will increase your productivity. When you do not look at your work day as a long, uphill battle, you will get more accomplished. Getting the tasks you dislike out of the way first, early in the day, will generate better results with all of your tasks. Not only will you get more done, you will be much more satisfied with the outcome of each and every task.

3. Increasing Motivation

"Be miserable, or motivate yourself. Whatever has to be done, it's always your choice"

We have all heard people say that they were "not motivated" as an excuse for not getting things done. In most cases, this is a polite way of saying that they are lazy. In the real world, where productivity and Success is essential, motivation is a key element. If it does not come naturally to you, you need to examine ways to increase your own motivation, and put it into action every day. The more motivated you are, the more things you are able to accomplish.

One of the most practical steps you can adopt to get your motivation up and running is to enjoy and appreciate your accomplishments. Applaud yourself for completing every single task, regardless big or small. While you should not be distracted or side-tracked from your main
focus, giving yourself the deserved credit as well as a figurative pat on the back will no doubt increase your motivation.

When you do this, it will also help to increase your stamina. Rather than feeling overwhelmed by one main goal on the horizon, which can leave you tired and stressed, it can make you feel more energetic and better prepared for the next task.

It is easy for a person to lose his sense of motivation when he feels that he is not accomplishing anything. This can result in him not feeling very good about what he does, and even doing less. Fortunately, it is not difficult to reverse this pattern and be back on track. When you get into the habit of feeling glad about every task you complete, and have pride in each and every accomplishment, it will increase your motivation to do even more, and to do better each time.

As motivation and energy are connected, you will also see that you have much more energy for all of the tasks in front of you. No matter how large your ultimate goal happens to be, or how much time and work you need to put into it to accomplish that particular goal, you will be pleasantly surprised at how much more smoothly it all progresses. As both your motivation and your energy increase, you will get more and more done. You will see how great productivity can be each day.

4. Setbacks Are Stepping Stones

Many people take setbacks negatively, and oftentimes your perception towards setbacks is the biggest obstacle and hindrance of productivity. When you focus on how setbacks can only bring you down and does not serve as a stepping-stone for you to move forward, you will end up not doing anything at all.

Setbacks occur in all areas of life. Regardless of what type of job you have, you probably experience them either occasionally or on a regular basis. Setbacks can occur from making mistakes, from not being adequately prepared for what you need to do, or from unexpected problems which are not anyone's fault. The way you experience and view a setback determines how it will affect you and your productivity. However a setback occurs, there is one outlook which can prevent it from becoming a roadblock, and actually increase your productivity.

Whether the setback was due to an error on your part, or whether it was no one's fault, refusing to see it as a failure is the first step in getting you back on track.

Another way of viewing setbacks is by perceiving them as an opportunity for you to do better next time. If you have made a mistake on your part, own up to it, correct the mistake and move on. There's no use of dwelling in the past as these can have repercussions.

You may beat yourself up about the mistake, or even obsess about it. These behaviors are never useful. Not only will they prevent you from getting things done, they will also cause you to feel bad about yourself. At its worst, it can lead you to feel incompetent. This is not the way to get things done.

Viewing each setback as a learning experience is the way to approach. Beating yourself up too much won't get you anywhere.

You should always remind yourself that you are capable of doing better, and capable of doing more. What you need to do is to correct the mistake, move on and make this pattern second nature to you. By doing this, setbacks will not bring you down and hinder your productivity.

5. Taking Care Of Yourself

If there's one thing we usually neglect to do, is taking care of our own physical wellbeing. If you are like most people, you have probably had the experience of working all night to get something done. You may have gone without sleep, skipped meals, and other important factors in self-care, for the purpose of finishing a task or meeting a deadline. While it is sometimes necessary to do this, neglecting self-care on a regular or frequent basis will backfire. Your health may suffer while you are not accomplishing nearly as much as you had hoped.

Many of us disregard the fact that taking care of our health will also keep
us productive. The person who goes without sleep on a regular basis, or relies on junk food instead of eating nutritious meals, will not be physically or mentally up to par. While you may believe that you are giving one hundred percent to your job, these unhealthy habits result in having less to give.

On the other hand, if you take care of yourself; getting sufficient sleep, keeping to a balanced diet, you will in turn contribute more to your work. When you are in top-notch condition, you will focus better, be more alert, and not become fatigued as easily. You will do better, and you will do more.

It is time to examine your lifestyle. Are you constantly depending on coffee or artificial energy boosters to keep you going? How about snacking on junk food? Are you getting enough sleep or are you constantly burning the midnight oil in order to complete your tasks? Try and reflect on these questions and if you find yourself leading an unhealthy lifestyle, it is high time for you to improve on it and observe how this has affected your day to day productivity.

Although nearly everyone is occasionally in the position of skipping a meal or working late into the night, if these have become habits for you it is not likely that they are helping you to become more productive. In fact, they are probably slowing you down.

Even if you have a fast-paced job with many responsibilities and deadlines, neglecting proper self-care is counterproductive. When you begin developing the habit of getting enough sleep and a proper diet, you will be doing more than taking care of yourself. You will get more done, and be more satisfied with the results. Always remember that overworking can backfire!

Chapter 8:
Use Leverage

Chapter 8: Use Leverage

When talking about productivity, few of us really tap into the power of leverage. We often hear the term 'leverage' when discussing investment and debt. However, leverage can be applied beyond that context, as it means to extend rewards or results and getting things done in a limited timeframe. When you have too much on your plate and you need to get things done as soon as possible, leverage is key.

The 3 Ways To Leverage:

- Duplicating

This can be applied in the context of creating products or future plans for your company. Many startup companies, waste their time and productivity by cracking their heads to invent new products.
The key here is to duplicate what already works or exists and improve on it. This will inevitably help you manage your resources better.

- Technology

We live in an era where almost anything can be automated, with the help of technology. For instance, you can automate your email, quote deliveries, presentations and even meeting notes. You just need to look up for the available platforms for you to do so.

Let's take your emails for example. You can easily set up your email client to create email templates (such as 'Canned Response' if you are using Gmail). If you need to send out emails at a specific time to a specific audience, you can schedule and set your email beforehand by using autoresponders; such as Aweber.

Automating can help you save a lot of time, especially if you are running your own business, as it can be very time consuming.Therefore, when you have automated all redundant tasks, you can focus on marketing and
scaling your business to greater heights.

- Outsourcing

Most business owners think they can handle everything on their own, but this can easily leave you overworked and overloaded. People also normally assume that as soon as you have established your own business or company, you need to hire full time employees and run an office. This will definitely incur great cost.

How do you leverage off a team excluding all the hassle of running a physical establishment and hefty costs? The answer is outsourcing. You have the capability to hire freelancers across the globe to create your products for you while you focus on marketing your business! This will help to increase your business's productivity.

Where do you search for freelancers?

There are various existing freelance websites to find the talents you need.

However, these are my top two picks:

1. Fiverr.com

Fiverr lets you buy or sell any service starting at a very reasonable rate of
$5. In Fiverr, a service is known as a 'Gig'. Fiverr is the world's largest marketplace for digital services. There is no need for you to negotiate pricing and the services offered are multiple of $5.

2. Upwork.com

Formerly known as ODesk, Upwork is a platform that connects clients with virtual freelancers. You can hire freelancers on an hourly basis or one off projects, depending on what needs to be done. What's different about Upwork is it's time tracking tool which makes it easy for you to track the project's progress and pay for the work they complete.

Let's take Uber for example. One of the most dominant growth factor for their company is their employment model, where they utilize freelancers to operate their business. This helps them to adapt to changes in demand effectively.

According to business.com, "freelancers are an essential asset in meeting the daily rigors of managing a startup. This is especially true for bootstrappers who don't necessarily have the resources to train or provide hardware for fresh hires" .

Therefore, what you need to do now is to list down which tasks you can manage on your own, and which you can delegate or outsource so you can immediately get down to business.

Chapter 9:
Follow One's Cause Until Successful (FOCUS)

Chapter 9: Follow One's Cause Until Successful

There is time enough for everything in the course of the day, if you do but one thing at once, but there is not time enough in the year, if you will do two things at a time." Lord Chesterfield

In the fast paced world we live in today, we are constantly on the go and multi-tasking has become second nature. Catching up with your work emails whilst driving, having lunch and preparing for that meeting.

Yes, we are able to do two or three tasks at once. But what's impossible is giving your full concentration to the multiple tasks at once.

Psychologists suggest that having fewer priorities and focusing on one task at a time leads to enhanced productivity. The brain struggles to transition from one task to another, simultaneously. This brain phenomenon is known as 'switching cost'.

Therefore the only solution for you is to focus. You need to make it a point to follow your cause until completed. Here are 5 tips for you to stay focused and concentrated on the task at hand:

1. Stop Multitasking, As Multitasking Is A Myth.

This is the first thing you need to sort out if you want to finish what you started.

Instead of rapidly switching between activities, commit to a single task at hand, focus on it until the end.

As stated earlier, it is possible for you to execute multiple tasks at hand, but that does not necessarily mean you are giving equal attention or concentration to each. Therefore, you may realize that the task completed would not be at par with what you expected it to be where you could actually perform better.

Doing more things at a time does not garner faster or better results. However, giving your undivided attention to one thing as best as you can, produces greater results. Many people mistaken productivity as getting a boatload of things done at a time. False. Why? Productivity is the measure of getting things done consistently.

2. Schedule Your Day, Plan Ahead

"People who plan to fail, fail to plan". As cliché as this may sound, it is indeed true. Sometimes, you have 1001 things to be completed within a day (which includes work, house chores, exercising and the list goes on). The only way for you to maintain your productivity level and Combat stress is by planning ahead.

Here are the two easy methods you can adopt in order to schedule your day and plan ahead:

3. Having A Planner To Amplify Your Productivity

Let's face it, we can be caught up with things that need to be done and sometimes, we forget what needs to be prioritized. Therefore, having a daily planner will work wonders for you.

Even though there are virtual planners made available for you out there, from Google calendar to your iPhone's planner, but let me suggest to you the best planner to use. The most practical and effective planner to keep you on track would be the traditional paper planner.

Why?

As paper planners gives you a visual and in your hand space for scribbling down notes whenever, wherever. Just imagine if you depend on your iPhone's planner and suddenly the battery dies out? Not that practical anymore.

Make sure you use the monthly view for important dates; such as birthdays, public holidays or special occasions. Use the weekly planning sections for more general tasks, such as visiting your grandparents by the end of the week, or mowing the lawn.

Meanwhile, for daily planning sections, you jot down specifically what you want to accomplish or what needs to be done for each day. This can be preparing for a meeting, going out with a friend or going to the gym.

This will inevitably help you to focus on what needs to be done and you are able to prioritize your workload. You can also prepare yourself for the tasks planned ahead. Your planner will also help in breaking down big or difficult tasks to smaller, manageable steps.

4. The Ivy Lee Method

If some of you are unfamiliar with this method, this method was established by a highly respected productivity consultant, known as Ivy Lee. This method was widely used since 1918 and proven effective to companies.

The Ivy Lee method comprises of 5 simple steps:

1.At the end of each working day, list down the six tasks you want to accomplish tomorrow. Do not exceed six tasks.

2.Prioritize these six tasks according to their importance.

3.When you start work the next day, place your focus solely on the first task on your list. Complete the first task before you move on to the next one.

4.Approach the rest of the task in the same fashion. Remember to only move on to the next task only when the previous task is completed.

5.Repeat this process every working day

This will no doubt help you stay focused on the task at hand, and will also boost your productivity.

5. Use The Pomodoro Technique

The Pomodoro Technique was invented back in the early 90s, by entrepreneur and author Francesco Cirillo. The method is fairly simple; when you need to complete large or multiple tasks, you break down the task into short time intervals. The most effective duration would be focusing on your task for a solid 25 minutes, and taking a short break of 5 minutes. The cycle repeats.

Using the Pomodoro Technique can help you charge through distractions, and it will help you focus to get things done in short intervals of time. It's an effective way to train your brain to pay full attention to the work you need to complete. This technique also enables you to take necessary breaks so you don't get burnt out or overwhelmed with the task at hand.

The Pomodoro technique ensures you are consistently productive and your motivation is kept in check by taking short breaks. All you need to do is to time yourself!

6. Eat Healthy To Retain Your Focus

One of the most important elements we take for granted is our eating habits. This contributes significantly to how our brain functions, which affects our attention span or focus.

In order to maximize your productivity and retain your focus, these are the dietary requirements or eating habits you may want to consider practicing; You need to keep the glucose level in your bloodstream steady. This helps your brain to focus for the long-term. This also fuels your brain and reserves the necessary energy needed for its mental functioning. Therefore, researchers suggest a low-glycemic diet. What does a low-glycemic diet consist of?

- Non-starchy vegetables

Leafy greens such as spinach, salads, broccoli and green beans.

- Nuts and seeds

Chia seeds, flax seeds, pumpkin seeds, almonds and walnuts.

- Beans and legumes

Soya beans or red beans. You should have this in small portions about half a cup per serving.

- Yoghurt and other fermented dairy

Greek or unsweetened yogurt, raw whole milk, traditionally made cheese.

- Whole grains

Oats, brown rice, wild rice, granola and muesli.

- Fresh fruits

Stone fruits, blueberries, cherries and citrus fruits.

- Healthy fats

Virgin coconut oil, extra virgin olive oil, nuts, seeds and avocado.

- Lean proteins

Salmon, turkey, skinless chicken breast, lamb and beef.

7. Meditate

Meditation does not only serve a spiritual purpose, but research has also proven that meditation can boost your attention span as well as keeping you focused on the task at hand.

You don't have to meditate at a monastery or on top of a mountain. All you need to do is invest at least 5 to 20 minutes of your time per day. Close your eyes and inhale deeply, preferably at a quite place so you are free from distractions. Think of nothing. You will see how your focus and attention span improves just after 4 days. Try and practice meditation first thing in the morning before you start your tasks.

Chapter 10: Conclusion

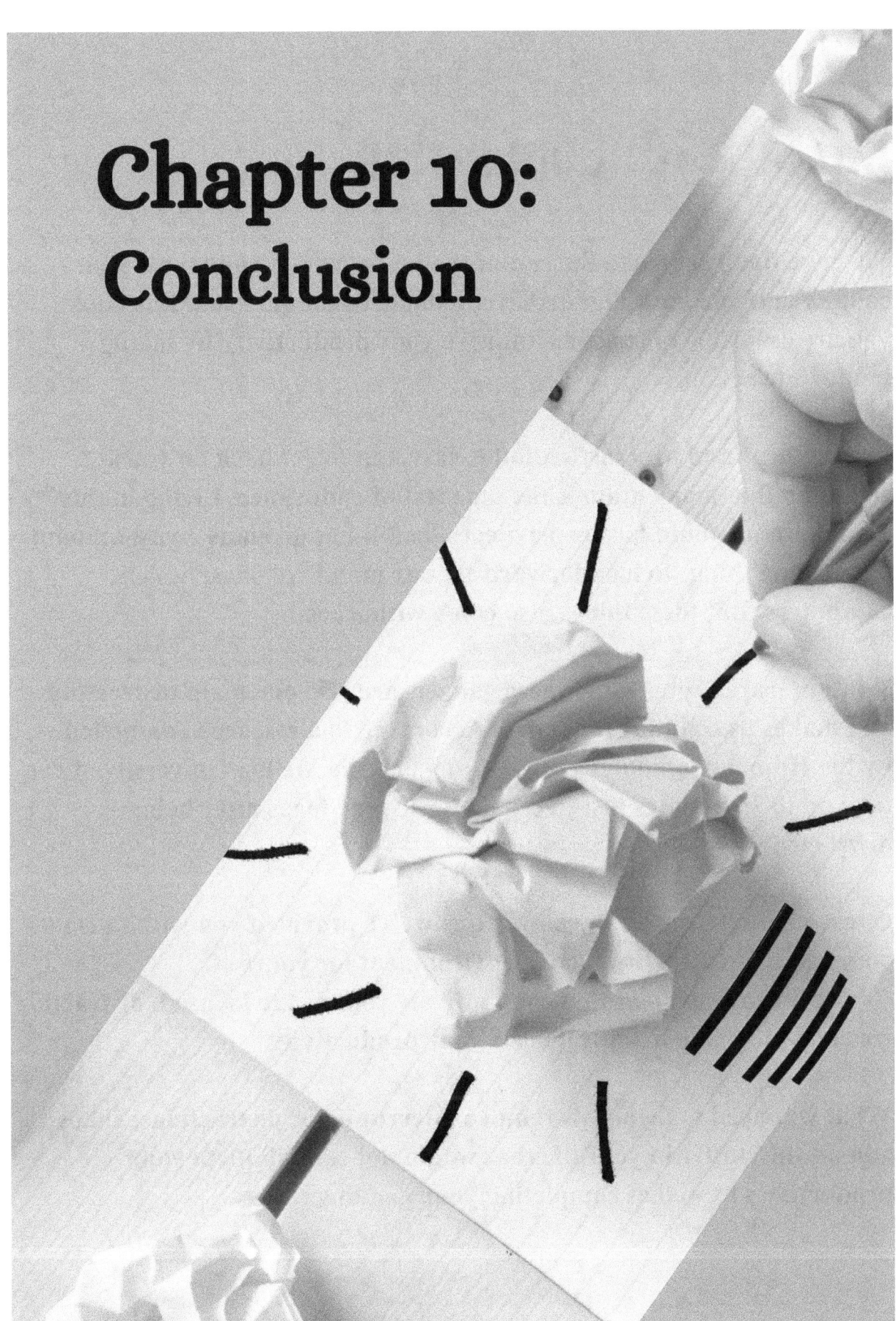

Chapter 10: Conclusion

We have finally come to the end of the book. Now is your time, your call. Even if you have digested every single technique from this book, you are only able to boost or improve your productivity by taking immediate action.

Losing focus and procrastination is easy, but to get back on track, retaining that momentum is the true test of endurance. Living in this digital era no doubt has its privileges, and it has given us a vast amount of amazing things to look forward to; our mobile phones, tablets, computers. But these things also come with a cost.

Without us realizing, all of these gadgets are also our main distractions and makes us counterproductive. According to a research conducted by the Human-Computer Institute at Carnegie Mellon University, it can take up to 25 minutes just to regain back your focus after being distracted.

Consequently, from all the power tips we've provided you with, it is now your job to create a productive environment for yourself.
Create an environment that can motivate you to stay focused, distraction free and most importantly, boosts your productivity.

What you need to do now is remove interruptions, distractions, chaos and all the clutter in your life that would not contribute to your productivity as well as completing your pending tasks.

Here's to supercharging your productivity!